PIANO SOLO

THE MODERN WEDDING COLLECTION

T0039795

ISBN 978-1-4950-4740-4

HAL•LEONARD®
CORPORATION
7777 W. BLUEMOUND RD. P.O. BOX 13819 MILWAUKEE, WI 53213

Visit Hal Leonard Online at
www.halleonard.com

ALL OF ME

Words and Music by JOHN STEPHENS
and TOBY GAD

Moderately slow, in 2

To Coda ⊕

D.S. al Coda

CODA

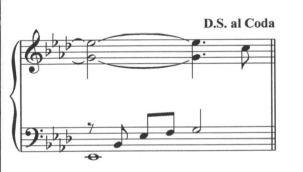

rit.

CLOSER

Words and Music by GREGORY KURSTIN,
SARA KEIRSTEN QUIN and TEGAN RAIN QUIN

To Coda

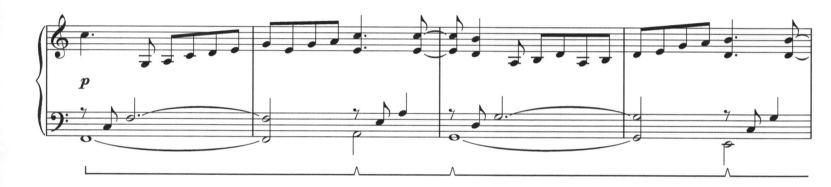

CODA

EVERYTHING

Words and Music by AMY FOSTER-GILLIES,
MICHAEL BUBLÉ and ALAN CHANG

Moderate groove

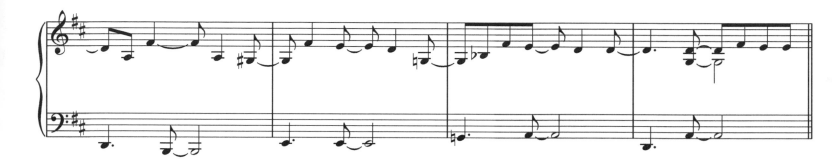

GOD GAVE ME YOU

Words and Music by
DAVE BARNES

Moderately

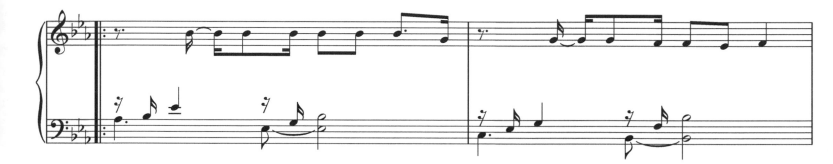

To Coda ⊕

D.S. al Coda

CODA

rit.

HOW LONG WILL I LOVE YOU

Words and Music by
MIKE SCOTT

Moderately

I WON'T GIVE UP

Words and Music by JASON MRAZ
and MICHAEL NATTER

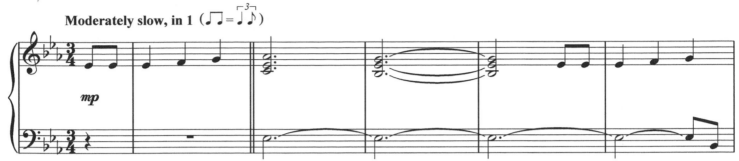

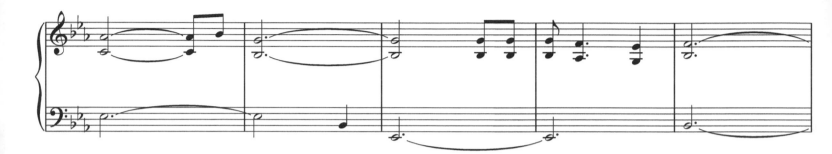

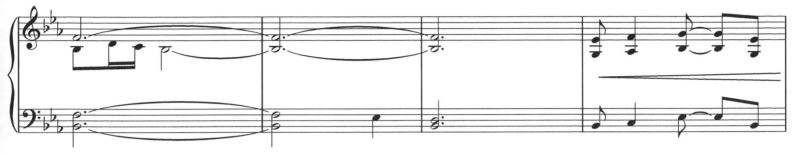

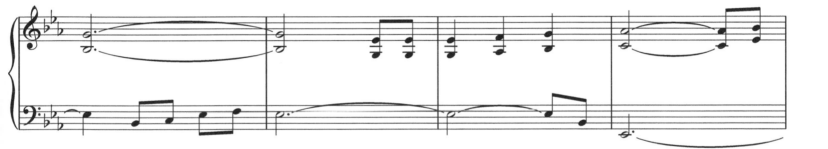

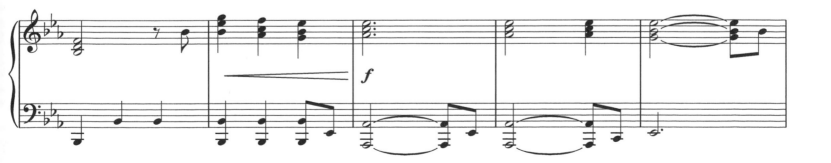

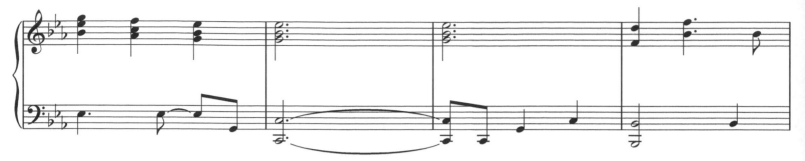

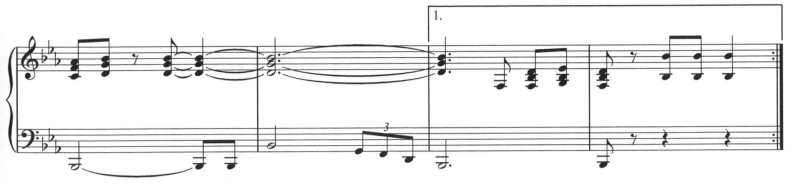

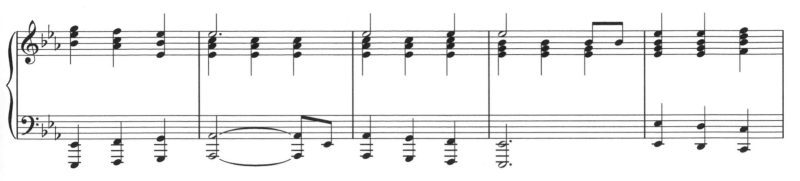

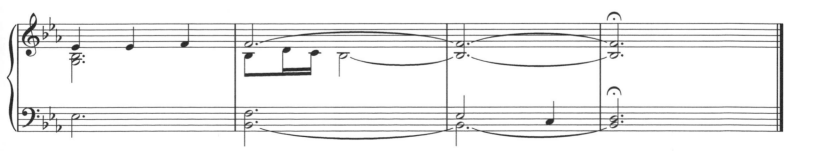

KISS ME

Words and Music by ED SHEERAN,
JULIE FROST, JUSTIN FRANKS
and ERNEST WILSON

Moderately slow

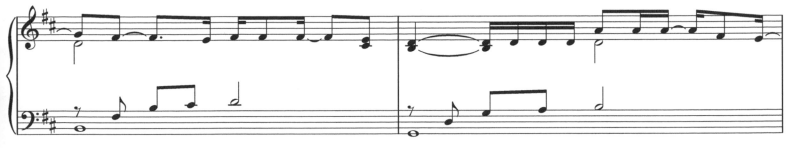

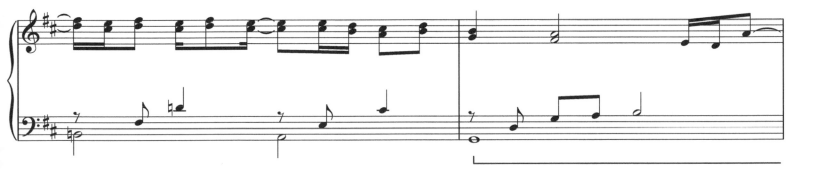

JUST THE WAY YOU ARE

Words and Music by BRUNO MARS,
ARI LEVINE, PHILIP LAWRENCE,
KHARI CAIN and KHALIL WALTON

Moderate Hip-Hop groove

To Coda ⊕

D.S. al Coda

CODA

LATCH

Words and Music by GUY LAWRENCE,
HOWARD LAWRENCE, JAMES NAPIER
and SAM SMITH

Moderately

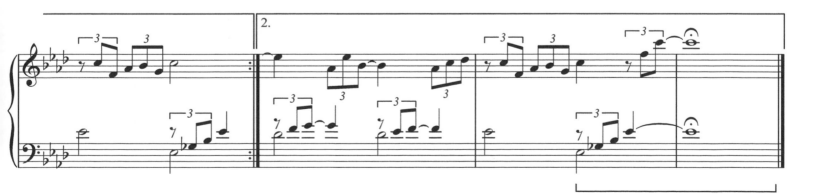

LOVE STORY

Words and Music by
TAYLOR SWIFT

Moderately

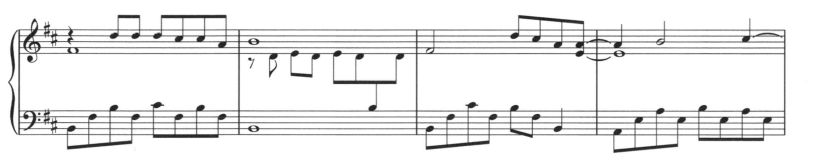

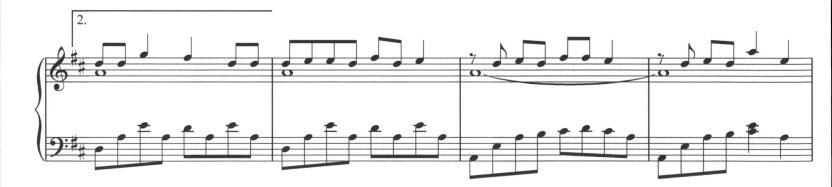

LOVE YOU LIKE THAT

Words and Music by CANAAN SMITH,
BRETT BEAVERS and JIM BEAVERS

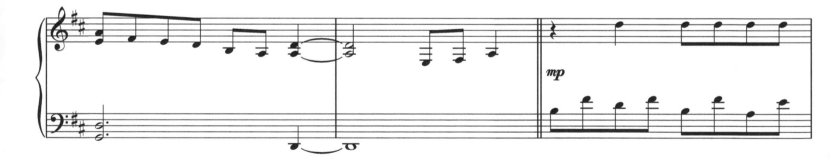

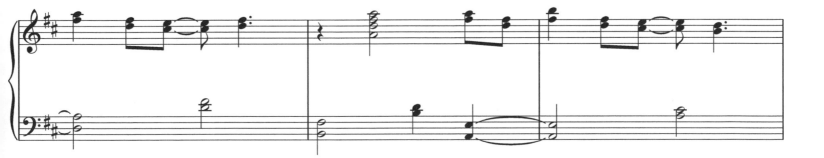

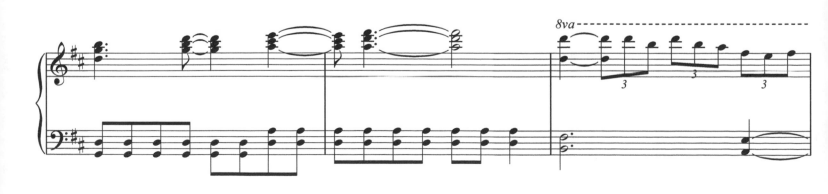

THE LUCKIEST

Words and Music by
BEN FOLDS

Slowly, in 2

LOVE ME LIKE YOU DO
from FIFTY SHADES OF GREY

Words and Music by MAX MARTIN,
SAVAN KOTECHA, ILYA,
ALI PAYAMI and TOVE LO

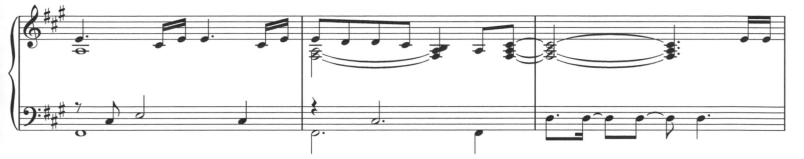

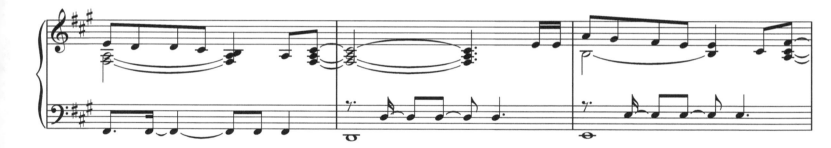

To Coda ⊕

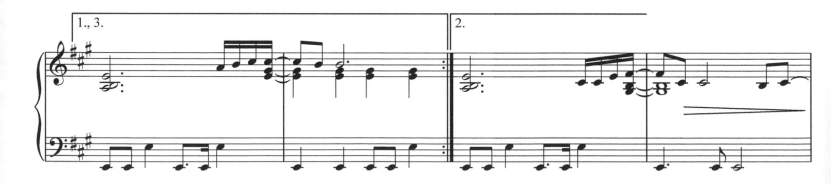

D.S. al Coda
(with repeat)

CODA

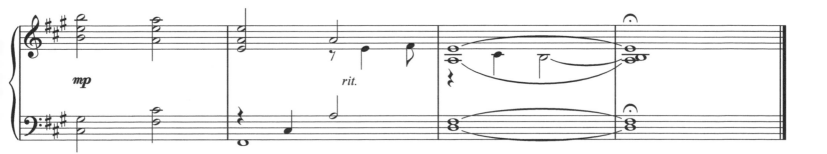

NO ONE

Words and Music by ALICIA KEYS,
KERRY BROTHERS, JR. and GEORGE HARRY

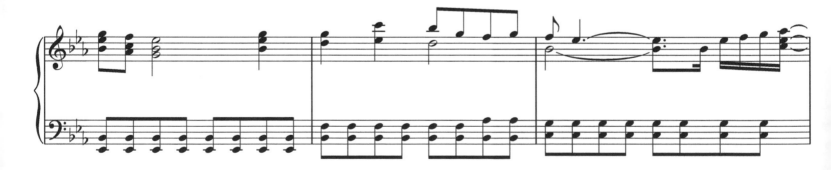

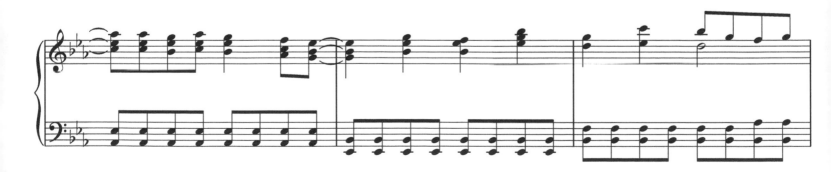

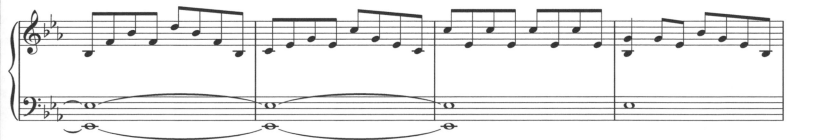

A SKY FULL OF STARS

Words and Music by GUY BERRYMAN,
JON BUCKLAND, WILL CHAMPION,
CHRIS MARTIN and TIM BERGLING

Moderately fast

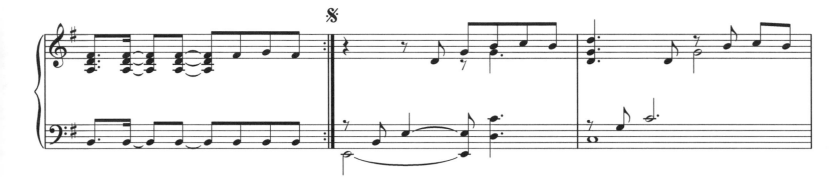

To Coda ⊕

D.S. al Coda

CODA

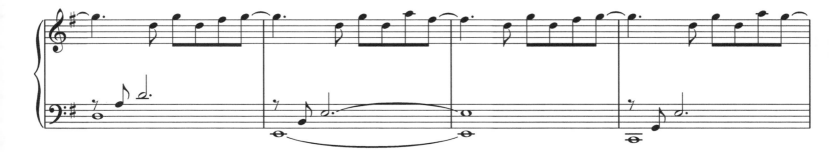

ONE AND ONLY

Words and Music by ADELE ADKINS,
DAN WILSON and GREG WELLS

With a bluesy shuffle

To Coda 𝄌

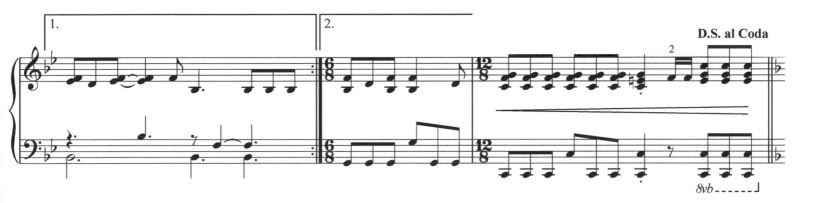

THINKING OUT LOUD

Words and Music by ED SHEERAN
and AMY WADGE

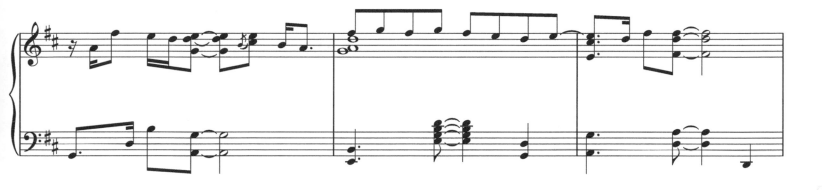

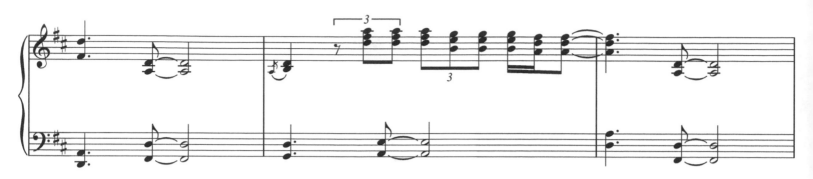

A THOUSAND YEARS

from the Summit Entertainment film THE TWILIGHT SAGA: BREAKING DAWN - PART I

Words and Music by DAVID HODGES
and CHRISTINA PERRI

Moderately slow, in 1

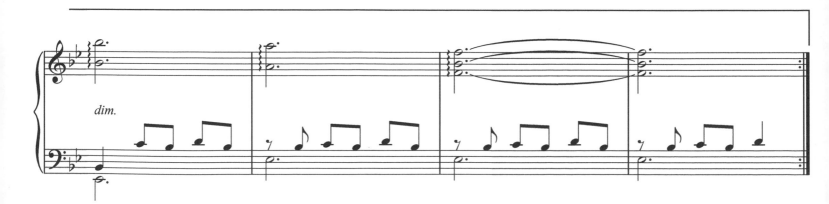

THE WAY I AM

Words and Music by
INGRID MICHAELSON

Moderately

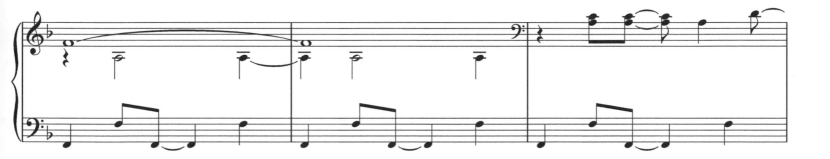

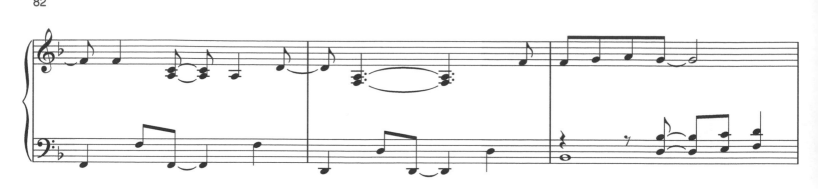

YOU'RE BEAUTIFUL

Words and Music by JAMES BLUNT,
SACHA SKARBEK and AMANDA GHOST

Moderately slow

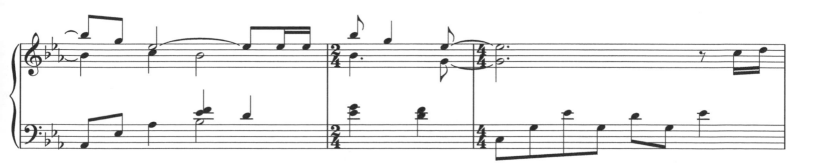

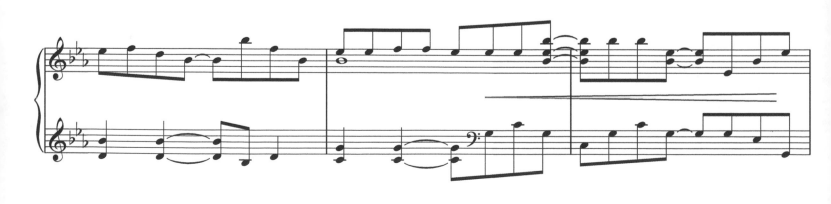

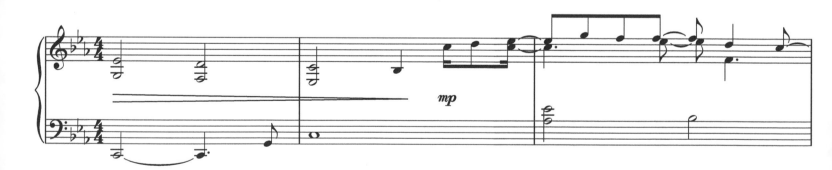

WE FOUND LOVE

Words and Music by
CALVIN HARRIS

Moderately fast

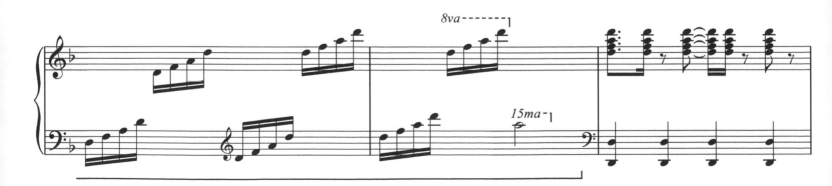

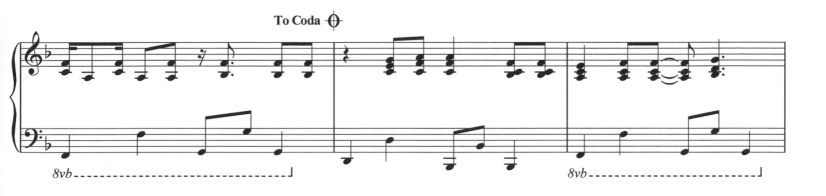

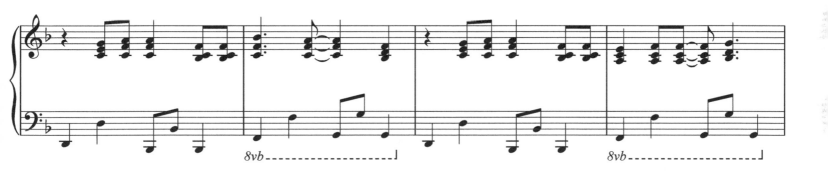

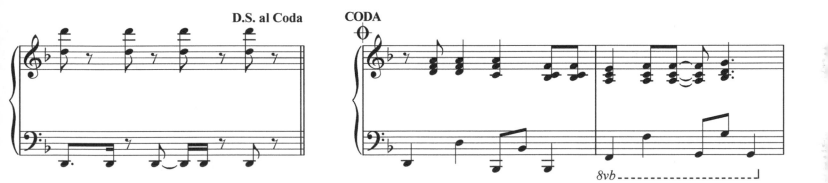

D.S. al Coda   **CODA**

YOUR FAVORITE MUSIC
ARRANGED FOR PIANO SOLO

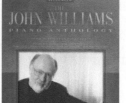

ARTIST, COMPOSER, TV & MOVIE SONGBOOKS

Adele for Piano Solo – 3rd Edition
00820186.............................. $19.99

The Beatles Piano Solo
00294023.............................. $17.99

A Charlie Brown Christmas
00313176.............................. $19.99

Paul Cardall – The Hymns Collection
00295925.............................. $24.99

Coldplay for Piano Solo
00307637.............................. $17.99

Selections from Final Fantasy
00148699.............................. $19.99

Alexis Ffrench – The Sheet Music Collection
00345258.............................. $19.99

Game of Thrones
00199166.............................. $19.99

Hamilton
00354612.............................. $19.99

Hillsong Worship Favorites
00303164.............................. $14.99

How to Train Your Dragon
00138210.............................. $22.99

Elton John Collection
00306040.............................. $24.99

La La Land
00283691.............................. $16.99

John Legend Collection
00233195.............................. $17.99

Les Misérables
00290271.............................. $22.99

Little Women
00338470.............................. $19.99

Outlander: The Series
00254460.............................. $19.99

The Peanuts® Illustrated Songbook
00313178.............................. $29.99

Astor Piazzolla – Piano Collection
00285510.............................. $19.99

Pirates of the Caribbean – Curse of the Black Pearl
00313256.............................. $22.99

Pride & Prejudice
00123854.............................. $17.99

Queen
00289784.............................. $19.99

John Williams Anthology
00194555.............................. $24.99

George Winston Piano Solos
00306822.............................. $22.99

MIXED COLLECTIONS

Beautiful Piano Instrumentals
00149926.............................. $19.99

Best Jazz Piano Solos Ever
00312079.............................. $27.99

Big Book of Classical Music
00310508.............................. $24.99

Big Book of Ragtime Piano
00311749.............................. $22.99

Christmas Medleys
00350572.............................. $16.99

Disney Medleys
00242588.............................. $19.99

Disney Piano Solos
00313128.............................. $17.99

Favorite Pop Piano Solos
00312523.............................. $17.99

Great Piano Solos
00311273.............................. $19.99

The Greatest Video Game Music
00201767.............................. $19.99

Most Relaxing Songs
00233879.............................. $19.99

Movie Themes Budget Book
00289137.............................. $14.99

100 of the Most Beautiful Piano Solos Ever
00102787.............................. $29.99

100 Movie Songs
00102804.............................. $32.99

Peaceful Piano Solos
00286009.............................. $19.99

Piano Solos for All Occasions
00310964.............................. $24.99

Sunday Solos for Piano
00311272.............................. $17.99

Top Hits for Piano Solo
00294635.............................. $16.99

HAL•LEONARD®
View songlists online and order from your favorite music retailer at
halleonard.com

THE BEST EVER
COLLECTION
ARRANGED FOR PIANO, VOICE AND GUITAR

150 OF THE MOST BEAUTIFUL SONGS EVER
00360735 150 ballads....................... $34.99

151 OF THE MOST BEAUTIFUL SONGS EVER
00291051 151 standards $49.99

BEST ACOUSTIC ROCK SONGS EVER
00310984 65 acoustic hits $29.99

MORE OF THE BEST ACOUSTIC ROCK SONGS EVER
00311738 69 songs.......................... $19.95

BEST BIG BAND SONGS EVER - 4TH EDITION
00286933 66 favorites....................... $19.99

BEST BLUES SONGS EVER
00312874 73 blues tunes.................. $19.99

BEST BROADWAY SONGS EVER - 6TH EDITION
00291992 85 songs........................... $29.99

MORE OF THE BEST BROADWAY SONGS EVER
00311501 82 songs........................... $22.95

BEST CHILDREN'S SONGS EVER - 2ND EDITION
00159272 101 songs......................... $19.99

BEST CHRISTMAS SONGS EVER - 6TH EDITION
00359130 68 holiday favorites.......... $29.99

BEST CLASSIC ROCK SONGS EVER - 3RD EDITION
00289313 64 hits.............................. $24.99

BEST CONTEMPORARY CHRISTIAN SONGS EVER 3RD EDITION
00289313 64 hits.............................. $24.99

THE BEST COUNTRY ROCK SONGS EVER
00118881 52 hits.............................. $19.99

BEST COUNTRY SONGS EVER - 3RD EDITION
00359135 76 classic country hits $27.99

BEST DISCO SONGS EVER
00312565 50 songs........................... $22.99

BEST EARLY ROCK 'N' ROLL SONGS EVER
00310816 74 songs........................... $19.95

BEST EASY LISTENING SONGS EVER - 4TH EDITION
00359193 75 mellow favorites.......... $24.99

BEST FOLK/POP SONGS EVER
00138299 66 hits.............................. $19.99

BEST GOSPEL SONGS EVER
00310503 80 gospel songs............... $22.99

BEST HYMNS EVER
00310774 118 hymns...................... $22.99

BEST JAZZ STANDARDS EVER - 3RD EDITION
00311641 77 jazz hits $24.99

BEST LATIN SONGS EVER - 3RD EDITION
00310355 67 songs........................... $24.99

BEST LOVE SONGS EVER - 3RD EDITION
00359198 62 favorite love songs...... $19.99

BEST MOVIE SONGS EVER - 5TH EDITION
00291062 75 songs........................... $24.99

BEST MOVIE SONGTRACK SONGS EVER
00146161 70 songs........................... $24.99

BEST POP/ROCK SONGS EVER
00138279 50 classics $19.99

BEST PRAISE & WORSHIP SONGS EVER
00311057 80 all-time favorites.......... $29.99

BEST ROCK SONGS EVER - 2ND EDITION
00490424 63 songs........................... $18.95

BEST SONGS EVER - 9TH EDITION
00265721 71 must-own classics $27.99

BEST STANDARDS EVER, VOL. 1 (A-L)
00359231 72 beautiful ballads.......... $17.95

BEST STANDARDS EVER, VOL. 2 (M-Z)
00359232 73 songs........................... $17.99

BEST WEDDING SONGS EVER - 2ND EDITION
00290985 70 songs........................... $27.99

HAL•LEONARD®

Visit us online
for complete songlists at
www.halleonard.com

Prices, contents and availability subject to change
without notice. Not all products available outside the U.S.A.